MUSIC FROM AROUND THE WORLD

FOR SOLO AND ENSEMBLE
VIOLA/VIOLIN 3
BY DONALD MILLER
MB21972

FREE Piano Accompaniment *AND* Ensemble score downloads are available online! *Visit: www.melbay.com/21972*

The solos in this book may be played in ensemble with the Violin 1/Violin 2 (21971) and Cello/Bass (21973) editions which are available for purchase.

Visit us on the Web at www.melbay.com or www.billsmusicshelf.com

INTRODUCTION

Many selections in this volume are unique and until now have been inaccessible to the string ensemble repertoire. Outstanding repertoire, representing several countries of the world, provide a great variety of ensemble selections. These pieces are intended for multiple strings for performance in the classroom as well as performance in concerts. Several players may be used on each part. Whenever possible, every effort was made to keep the viola and violoncello/double bass parts melodic rather than simply filling in the various harmonic chord progressions. The pieces may be performed as a solo for each instrument (Violin 1, Violin 2, Viola or Cello) with piano accompaniment, or as duets or trios, as well as full orchestra. If performed with full orchestra, the piano accompaniment is not necessary.

The string ensemble series meets all standards for ASTA with NSOA (American String Teachers Association/National School Orchestra Association) and Suzuki Association of the Americas, Inc.

Full Orchestra Score

If performed with full orchestra, no solo parts should be played except the 1st violin part. Note also, if you wish to perform these works with full orchestra and you are short certain instruments; you still have some flexibility with the score. For example, if there are not enough violas for balance, the viola (harmony part) and 3rd violin part are identical. Please Note: standard string terminology is used. // = bow change (lift and release); , = standard pause.

Combining Ensembles

If a guitar class is available, both string and guitar class participants may be combined for performance. (Donald Miller Guitar Ensemble Series – Music from Around the World - MB98304.) Identical keys and repertoire are used in both the String Ensemble and Guitar Ensemble Series. All keys are guitar and string friendly.

A word of gratitude to Peter Ciarelli for the beautiful work he did in preparing the manuscripts on Finale software for publication. Special thanks to my wife, Mary for all her help.

I am most grateful for the bowings and string articulation suggestions by William J. Mercer. Mr. Mercer completed his undergraduate studies at the Crane School of Music and his Masters degree in Musicology from Syracuse University. Before retiring, he spent 30 years teaching orchestral music in the Liverpool Central School District (New York). Mercer is an active guest conductor, adjudicator, clinician and consultant. He is a past President of the New York State School Music Association and currently is an adjunct professor of the Music Education Department of Ithaca College.

Sincerely,

Don Miller

To: Peter Ciarelli

CONTENTS

About the Author

Don Miller was an award-winning jazz guitarist while a student at the University of Cincinnati College-Conservatory of Music. The guitarist placed first at the University of Notre Dame Jazz Festival and recorded an LP with his quartet, which received three stars in Downbeat. He received his DMA from the University of Southern California in 1981. His Finger Lakes Suite was premiered by the Syracuse Symphony Orchestra in 1989. In addition, the author has many published choral compositions and conducted award-winning choral groups at Onondaga Community College and Le Moyne College in Syracuse, NY. In 1991, he received New York State's highest award, the SUNY Chancellor's Award for Excellence in Teaching as well as the NISOD Excellence Award from the University of Texas at Austin. He is professor emeritus of Music at Onondaga Community College and is retired from Le Moyne College.

Amor Vittorioso

Love Victorious

Amor Vittorioso

Love Victorious

Amor Vittorioso

Love Victorious

Arirang

Lullaby

Arirang

Lullaby

Arirang

Lullaby

Korean Folk Song
Arr. Don Miller

Violin III

Hatikvah and Shalom Chaverim

The Hope and Farewell Friends

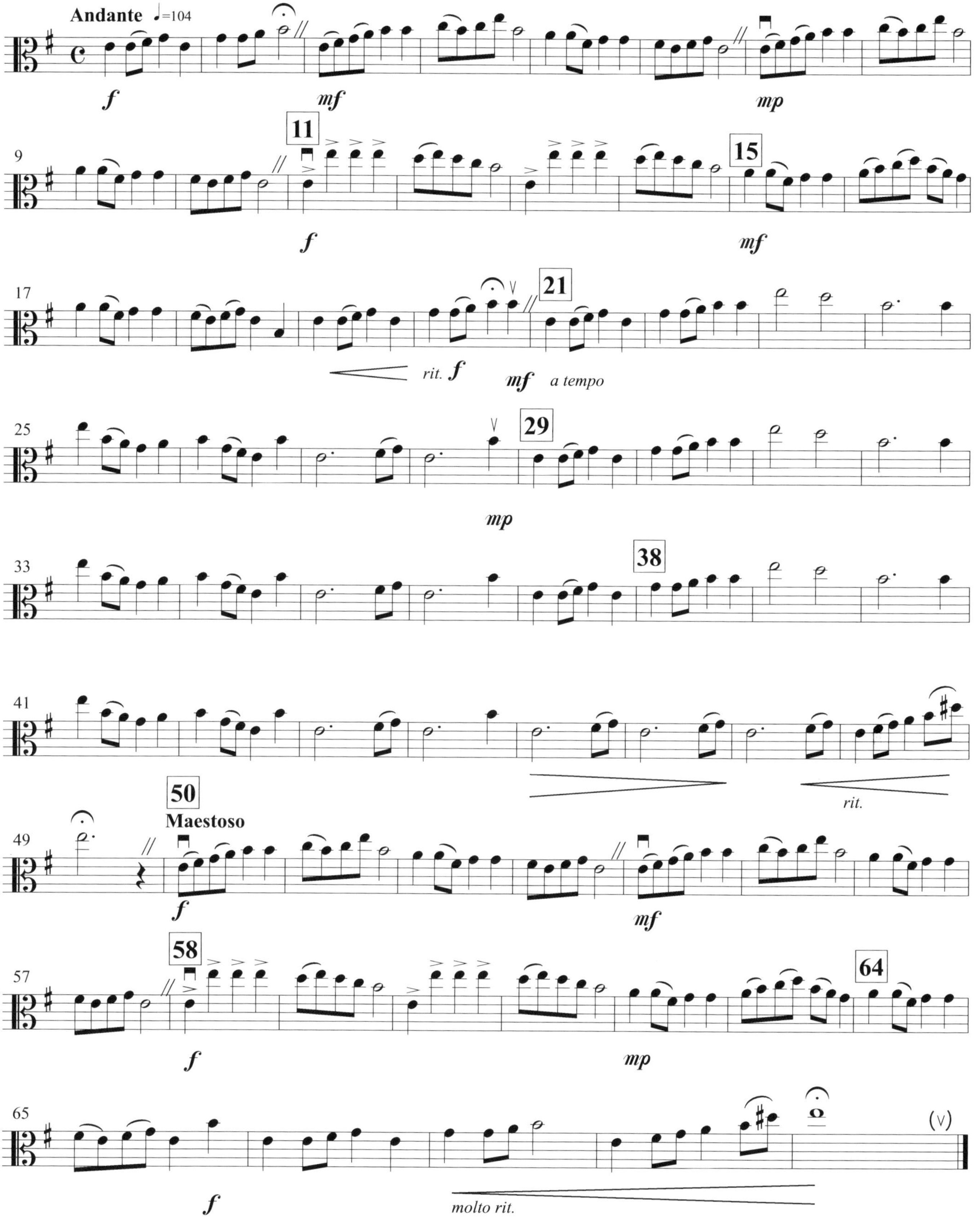

Hatikvah and Shalom Chaverim

The Hope and Farewell Friends

Traditional Hebrew Melodies
Arr. Don Miller

Viola

Hatikvah and Shalom Chaverim

The Hope and Farewell Friends

Traditional Hebrew Melodies
Arr. Don Miller

Violin III

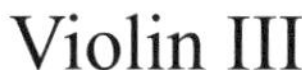

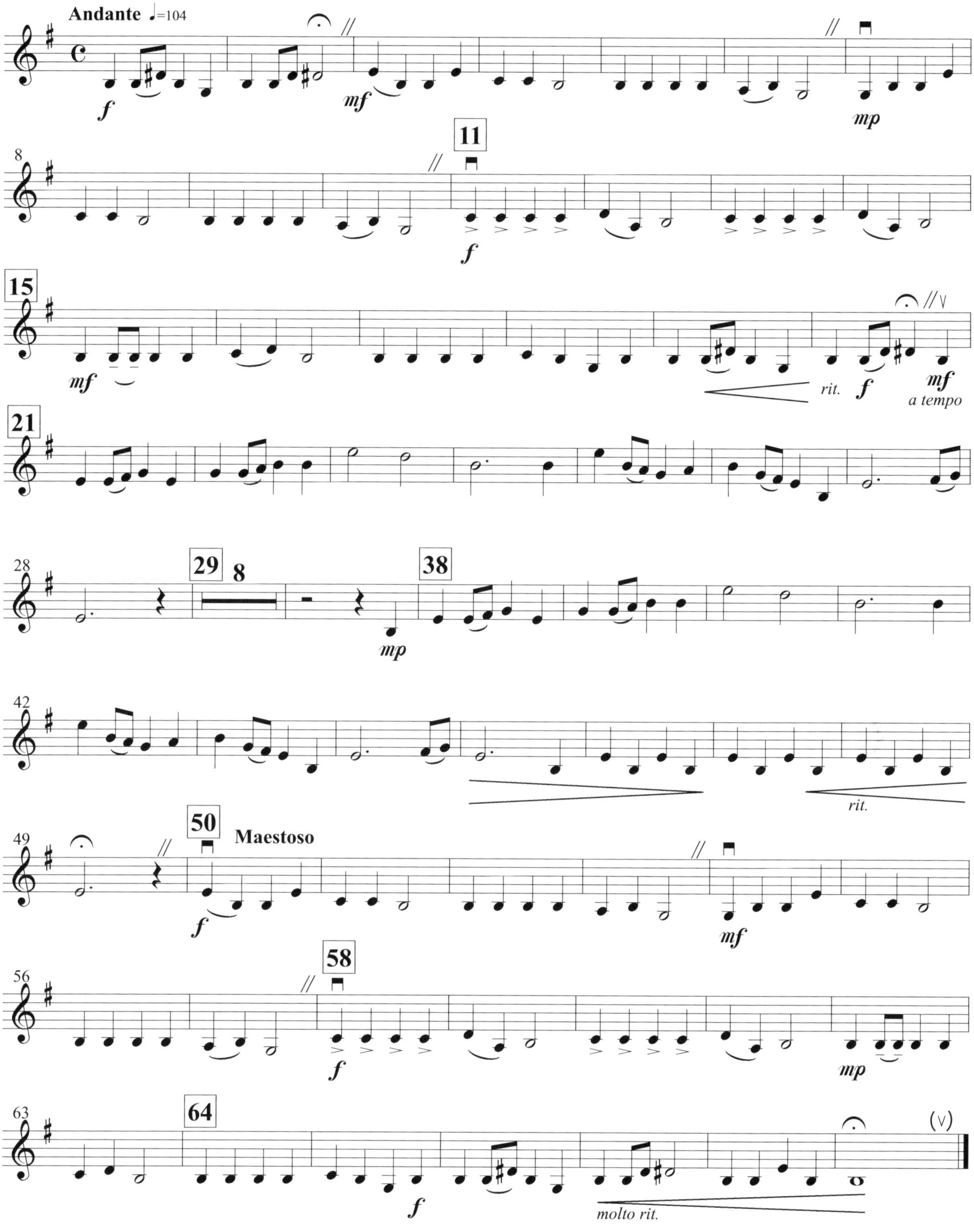

John Anderson, My Jo

John Anderson, My Jo

John Anderson, My Jo

Scottish Folk Song
Arr. Don Miller

Violin III

Three Jolly Welshmen

Three Jolly Welshmen

Three Jolly Welshmen

The Streets of Laredo

The Streets of Laredo

The Streets of Laredo

Violin III

This page left blank to avoid awkward page turn.

Neighbors' Chorus

from the French Comic Opera La jolie Parfumeuse

Jacques Offenbach
1819-1880
Arr. Don Miller

Viola (Melody)

Viola (Melody)

Neighbors' Chorus
from the French Comic Opera La jolie Parfumeuse

Jacques Offenbach
1819-1880
Arr. Don Miller

Viola

Viola
55
60
62
rit.
68
mp
a tempo
76
75
83
85
f
rit.
p
a tempo
89
93
94
mf
100
piu mosso (in one)
f
106
108
f
mp
f
27

Neighbors' Chorus

from the French Comic Opera <u>La jolie Parfumeuse</u>

Jacques Offenbach
1819-1880
Arr. Don Miller

Violin III

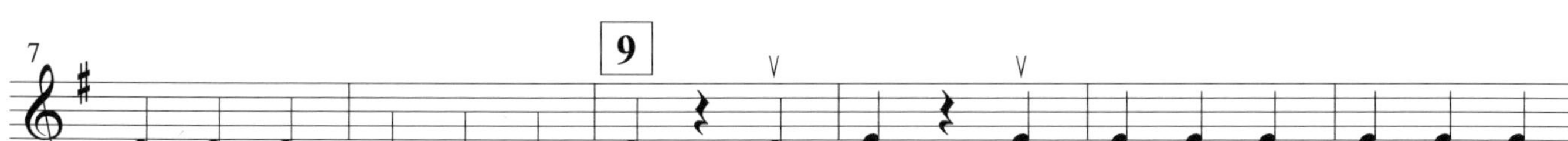

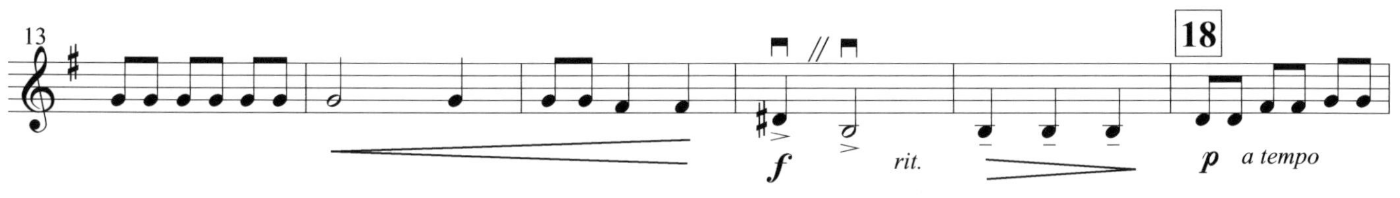

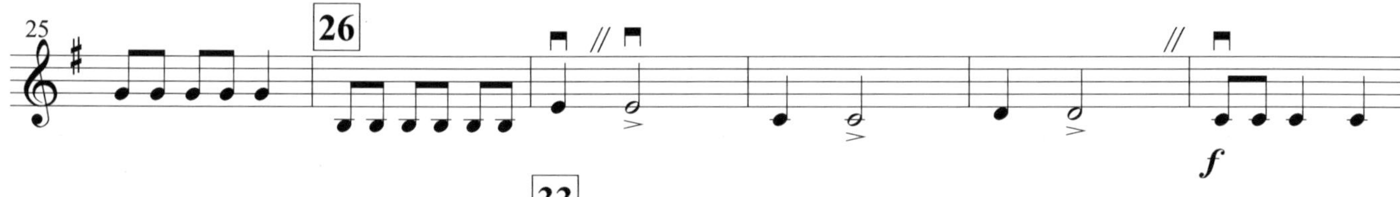

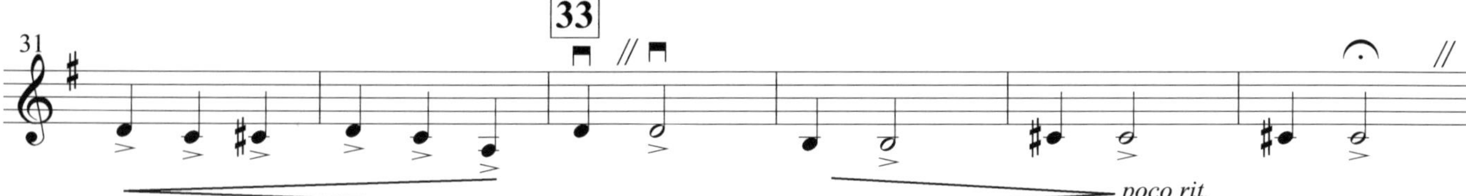

28

Violin III

55
60
f
mp
f
62
rit.
68
mp
a tempo
75
76
83
85
f
rit.
p
a tempo
89
93
94
mf
100
piu mosso (in one)
f
106
108

A Pretty Little Ring

Norwegian Folk Song
Arr. Don Miller

A Pretty Little Ring

Norwegian Folk Song
Arr. Don Miller

31

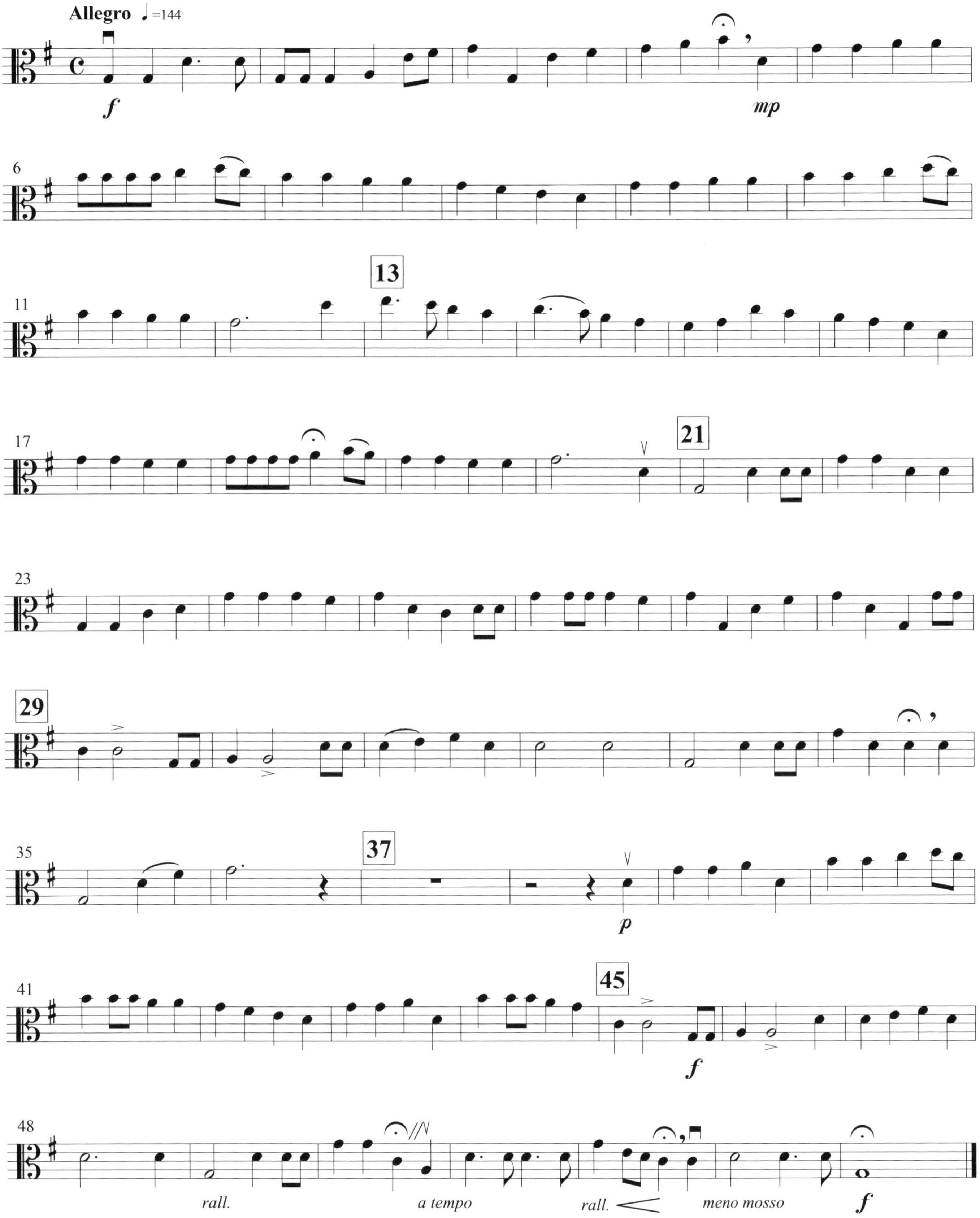

A Pretty Little Ring

Violin III

Norwegian Folk Song
Arr. Don Miller

Tina Singu

We Are the Flame

Viola (Melody)

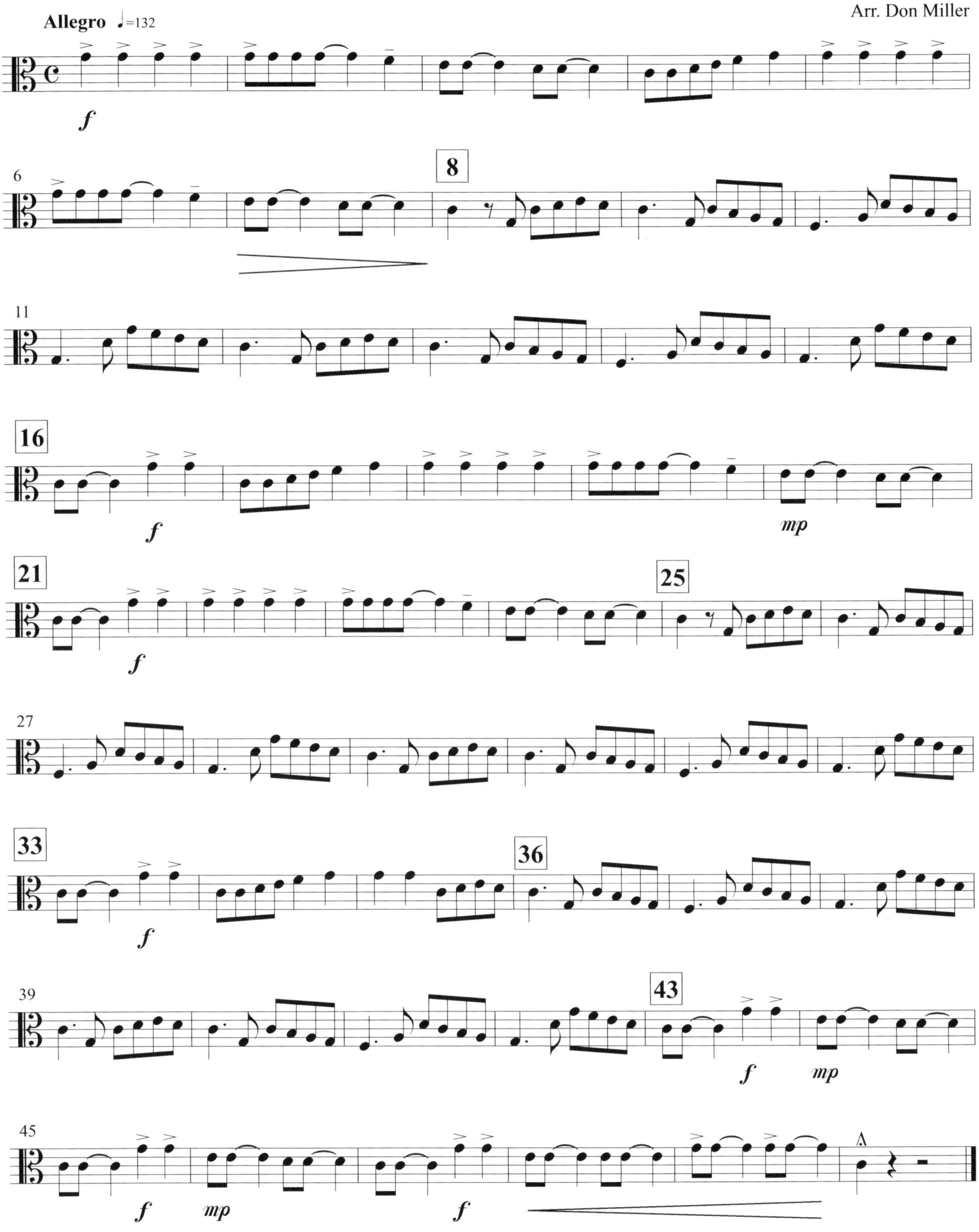

Tina Singu

We Are the Flame

Viola

Allegro ♩=132

Basutoland Folk Song
Lesotho, South Africa
Arr. Don Miller

Tina Singu

We Are the Flame

Basutoland Folk Song
Lesotho, South Africa
Arr. Don Miller

Violin III

Allegro ♩=132

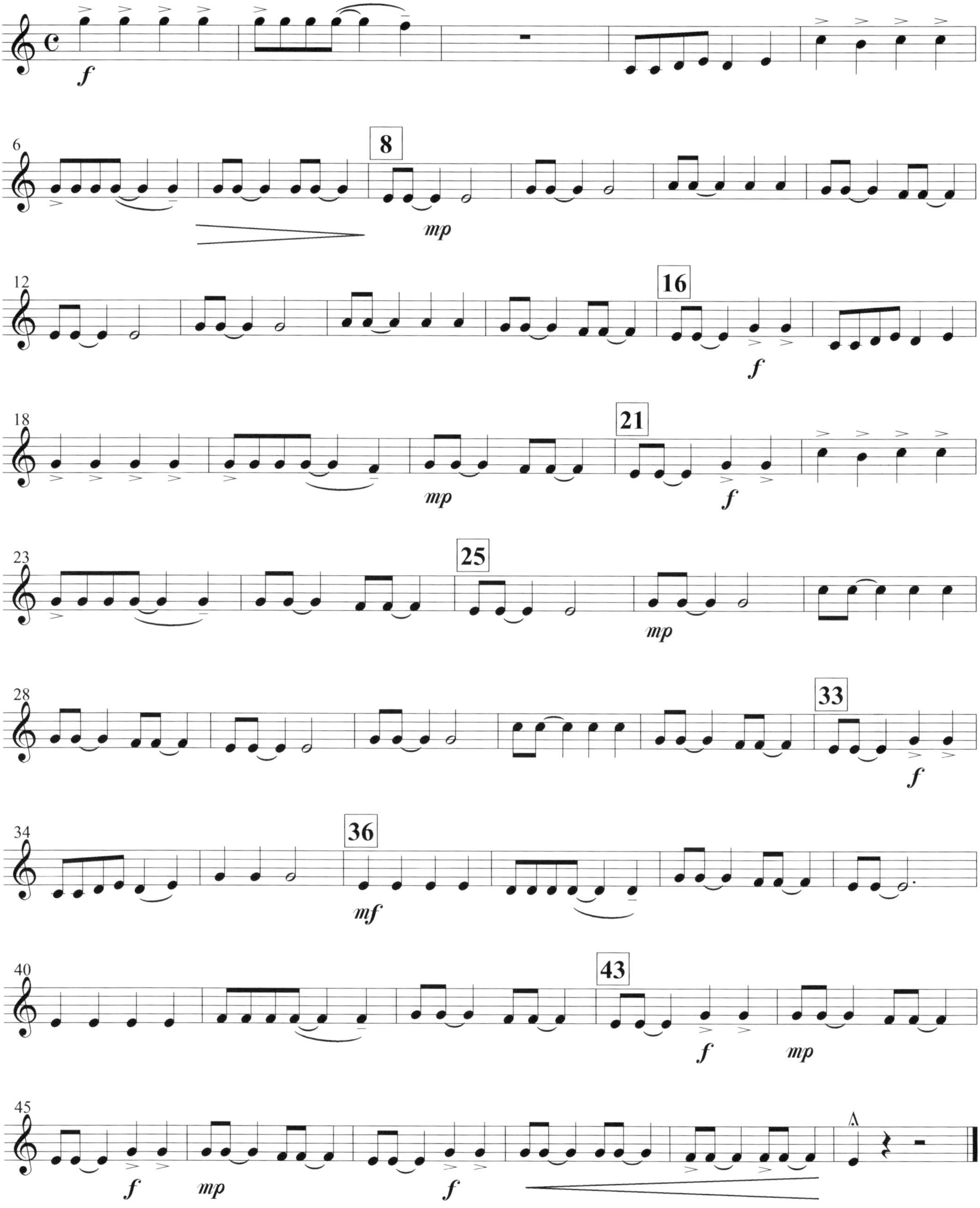

O'er Wintry Hills

O'er Wintry Hills

O'er Wintry Hills

Notes:

Made in the USA
Monee, IL
07 July 2026